POPULAR PET CARE

Turtles

Ann Larkin Hansen
ABDO & Daughters

Pets are more than just toys or playthings. They are part of our families. It is important to love and care for them. Popular Pet Care will help you understand your pet and know of its unique needs. Remember that your pet will depend on you to be responsible in caring for it.

Dr. David C. Hallstrom—Veterinarian

Published by Abdo & Daughters, 4940 Viking Drive, Suite 622, Edina, Minnesota 55435.

Copyright © 1997 by Abdo Consulting Group, Inc., Pentagon Tower, P.O. Box 36036, Minneapolis, Minnesota 55435 USA. International copyrights reserved in all countries. No part of this book may be reproduced in any form without written permission from the publisher.

Printed in the United States.

Cover Photo by: Vik Orenstein
Interior Photos by: Vik Orenstein, Peter Arnold, Super Stock
Illustrations and Icons by: C. Spencer Morris

Edited by Lori Kinstad Pupeza
Contributing editor Dr. David C. Hallstrom—Veterinarian

Special thanks to our Popular Pet Care kids:
Peter Dumdei, Gracie Hansen, Brandon Isakson, Laura Jones, Annie O'Leary, Peter Rengstorf, Morgan Roberts, Tyler Wagner, and Shane Wagner.

Library of Congress Cataloging-in-Publication Data

Hansen, Ann Larkin.
     Turtles / Ann Larkin Hansen.
     p.   cm. -- (Popular pet care)
     Includes Index.
     Summary: Provides information about turtles and how to feed and care for, house and handle them, and keep them as pets.
     ISBN 1-56239-784-2
     1. Turtles as pets--Juvenile literature. [1. Turtles as pets. 2. Pets.]
     I. Title. II. Series: Hansen, Ann Larkin. Popular pet care.
     SF459.T8H36   1997
     639.3'92--dc21
                                     97-6054
                                       CIP
                                       AC

Contents

Why Have
A Turtle?

If you're looking for a pet that's really different, try turtles. Turtles are **reptiles**, and they do things differently than other pets. They eat underwater and lay their eggs on land. They can't hear you, but they can smell you and feel you scratching their shell.

Turtles have no teeth. The females can be twice as big as the males. Many turtles **hibernate** in cold weather.

Turtles have been around since the dinosaurs lived on the earth. Turtles haven't changed for 200 million years. And a pet turtle can live a long, long time—20 to 50 years, or more.

**Turtles make
great pets.**

Warning!

Turtles often carry the **Salmonella bacteria**. It doesn't bother the turtles, but it can make you very sick. To stay healthy, always follow these rules:

Always wash your hands with soap and hot water after handling your turtles.

Never let your turtle in the kitchen or bathroom, or near any human food.

Never wash your turtle pen or dishes in the kitchen or bathroom sink. Use the basement sink or an outside hose.

Pregnant women and kids under five years old should not handle turtles. If you have cuts or sores on your hands, wear plastic gloves to handle your turtle.

Opposite page: Always handle turtles with care.

Kinds of Turtles

There are about 250 **species** of turtles in the world, but only about six kinds that make good pets for beginners. **Painted turtles**, **musk turtles**, **mud turtles,** and **pond turtles** are all native to the United States and stay small enough to keep in an **aquarium**. **Reeve's turtles** are from China and Japan. **Box turtles** live on land instead of in the water, and need a special pen.

Get two turtles, since they like company. Pick a turtle that is alert and active, and feels heavy. A **captive-bred** turtle is more likely to be healthy than one taken from the wild.

Painted turtle

Box turtle

Getting Ready
for Turtles

For **water turtles**, start with a 30-gallon or bigger **aquarium** that is longer and wider than it is high. Don't use any gravel or sand on the bottom. Put in some smooth rocks or a piece of driftwood so your turtles can get completely out of the water and dry off. This is called the basking spot.

If you have female turtles, they will need a land area for laying eggs. You will need an adult to help wall off part of the aquarium with plexiglass and silicone glue. Fill this area with dirt or sand.

A turtle aquarium.

Heat, Light, and Filters

Fill the **aquarium** with water that is deeper than your turtles are wide. This lets a turtle flip over and keep from drowning if it gets turned upside down.

Buy a strong filter from the pet store to keep the water clean. You will also need a water heater to keep the water between 75° F (24° C) and 85° F (29° C) degrees. A thermometer will let you know if the temperature is right.

You will need two lights for your turtle tank. A Vitalite™ gives imitation sunlight, which turtles need to stay healthy. Shine a clip-on lamp on the basking area at a distance that will keep the temperature between 85° F (29° C) and 90° F (32° C) degrees.

You can buy an aquarium at a pet store.

Taking Care
of Turtles

Get your tank up and running before you bring turtles home. Make sure the filters, lights, and heaters are all working, and that the temperatures are right.

Once your turtles are home, keep the lights on about 12 hours a day. If you have a good filter and feed your turtles in a separate dishpan full of water, the tank will stay fairly clean. You will only have to change half the water every week. Clean the filter also. Every month, take the tank apart completely and scrub it, using a mild cleaner. Once a year, put in a new Vitalite™.

Cleaning your aquarium
is an important job.

Feeding Turtles

Turtles are **omnivores**, eating both plants and animals. Adults need to eat half plants and half animals. Young turtles need to eat more animals than plants.

Feed adult turtles every other day, and young turtles every day. Feed them only as much as they can eat in a few minutes, or they will get fat. Turtles are very messy. Feed them in a separate container full of water.

Turtles need lots of variety in their diet. Feed adults about one-fourth Tetra Reptomin or Purina Trout Chow from the pet store. Fish, cooked chicken, bugs, and worms should make up another fourth. Half of the feed should be fresh vegetables, fruit, or other plants.

Turtles eat both plants and animals.

Vitamins and Minerals

Turtles need a lot of **calcium** to keep their bones and shells healthy. Give them either a piece of **cuttlebone** or a block of plaster of paris to gnaw. Turtles also need direct sunlight to make vitamin D3, which allows their bodies to use the calcium.

Don't put your **aquarium** in the sun. You will cook your turtle. Some turtles like to go outside for walks, but others hate it and will quit eating.

The best way to make sure your turtle gets the **vitamins** it needs is to use a Vitalite™, and add bird or **reptile** vitamins to the food. Some owners mix powdered vitamins into the plaster of paris.

A box turtle eating strawberries.

Turtle Behavior and Health

Turtles behave so differently from other pets that sometimes it is hard to tell if they are sick or not. Some turtles will quit eating for weeks, and then start again as if nothing has happened. But a turtle will also quit eating if it is too cold, and can starve to death.

It's normal for a turtle to shed its skin once in a while, or to sneeze. But if a turtle is gasping, tilted when it's swimming, or has a runny nose or swollen eyes, it is probably sick. Call a **reptile veterinarian** any time your turtle looks or acts differently than usual. It may be nothing, but it's best to check.

A turtle swimming in its aquarium.

Keeping Turtles Outside

Turtles love spending the summer outside. Put them in a kid's plastic swimming pool or other big container. Set up a basking spot and a land area. A flowerpot on its side or some other hiding spot is also needed.

The pen should have at least two full hours of sunlight each day. There should also be a shaded area for when your turtle gets hot.

If your turtles are small, put mesh over the pen to keep them from being carried away by cats, dogs, birds, or raccoons. Keep the water clean by changing it regularly and feeding your turtles in a separate container.

Turtles like to bask in the sun.

Box Turtles

Unlike other pet turtles, American **box turtles** live on land and can't swim. They need a clean water dish for drinking and wading, and a temperature of about 75° F (24° C). A Vitalite™ is also necessary. A box turtle table can be built with adult help out of plexiglass and plywood.

Box turtles are terrific climbers and diggers, so pens need to have sides more than a foot high. They like to hide in hollow logs or flowerpots, and should have plenty of moist dirt to dig. Box turtles especially like hunting down bugs and worms, and living in groups.

Opposite page: A brightly colored box turtle.

Finding Out More About Turtles

Each type of turtle has different needs. **Painted turtles** will bask all day, but **mud turtles** hardly ever bask. **Reeve's turtles** seem to eat anything, but **musk turtles** need to eat more meat and can be finicky. To keep your turtle happy and healthy, you need to find out as much as possible about it. There are not many books on turtles, but there is a lot of information on the internet.

As you get better at taking care of turtles, you may want to try hatching eggs, or letting your turtles **hibernate**. You could try keeping some of the larger or more difficult types of turtles. Turtles could keep you interested for the rest of your life!

When Turtles Die

Some big turtles live longer than people. But the small turtles we keep as pets live from about 5 to 25 years. It all depends on what kind of turtle you have, how healthy it is, and how well it's cared for.

But one day your pet will die of sickness or old age. It's okay to feel sad about losing your pet. But you can be proud of yourself if you gave your turtle a happy life, with plenty of clean water, warm sun, and interesting food.

Wrap the body in a plastic bag and put it in the garbage. Clean and disinfect the turtle tank and equipment, and your hands. A friend or relative may want your equipment for their pet turtle. Or you might remember how neat it is to have a turtle, and want to have another one!

*Turtles are
great pets.*

Glossary

Aquarium: a glass-sided tank built to hold water.

Bacteria: microscopic organisms. There are millions of different kinds, some of which cause illness in animals and humans.

Box turtle: a land turtle that grows to seven inches or less and lives for 40 to 50 years.

Calcium: a chemical element necessary for strong bones and shells.

Carapace: the top part of a turtle's shell. Turtles are measured by the length of their carapace.

Captive-bred: born and raised in captivity instead of captured in the wild.

Cuttlebone: bone from the ocean cuttlefish. It's sold in pet stores.

Hibernate: to spend winter in a dormant state, not eating or moving, and hardly breathing.

Mud turtle: a small, secretive turtle that grows to five or six inches. They are bottom feeders, and active mostly at night.

Musk turtle: very similar to the mud turtle, but even smaller. Needs more animal foods than other turtles.

Omnivore: eats all types of food. A carnivore eats only meat, and an herbivore eats only plants.

Painted turtle: a shy turtle that loves to bask and grows up to ten inches long. Painted turtles must be kept very clean. It can live for up to 25 years.

Plastron: the bottom part of a turtle's shell.

Pond turtle: a turtle from the Pacific coast that grows to less than seven inches. This turtle spends almost all its time in the water.

Reeve's turtle: A tame, hardy turtle from China and Japan. It grows to about 5 inches, and tends to be very active during the day.

Reptile: a class of cold-blooded animals that includes snakes, lizards, crocodiles, and turtles. Reptiles can't produce their own heat to stay warm, so they depend on sunlight and warm temperatures.

Reptile Veterinarian: an animal doctor that specializes in reptile care.

Salmonella: a type of rod-shaped bacteria. There are many different varieties, and it can cause many different illnesses.

Scutes: the outer covering, or scales, of the turtle's shell.

Species: a distinct type of plant or animal.

Vitamins: organic substances found in foods, and necessary for good health. Some vitamins are manufactured by the body. Vitamin D3 is made when skin is exposed to sunlight, and this vitamin allows calcium to be deposited in bone.

Water turtle: a turtle that spends much of its life in the water.

Index